What

Teacher's Choice Series

Toni M. Egan
Davis, California

Illustrations by
Steve Pileggi

Dominie Press, Inc.

The development of the *Teacher's Choice Series* was supported by the Reading Recovery project at California State University, San Bernardino. All authors' royalties from the sale of the *Teacher's Choice Series* will be used to support various Reading Recovery projects.

Publisher: Raymond Yuen
Series Editor: Stanley L. Swartz
Illustrator: Steve Pileggi
Cover Designer: Steve Morris
Page Design: Michael Khoury

Published by:

Dominie Press, Inc.

1949 Kellogg Avenue
Carlsbad, California 92008 USA

ISBN 1-56270-569-5
Printed in Singapore by PH Productions Pte Ltd.
2 3 4 5 6 IP 99 98 97

What if I were

as high as a kite,

as slow as a snail,

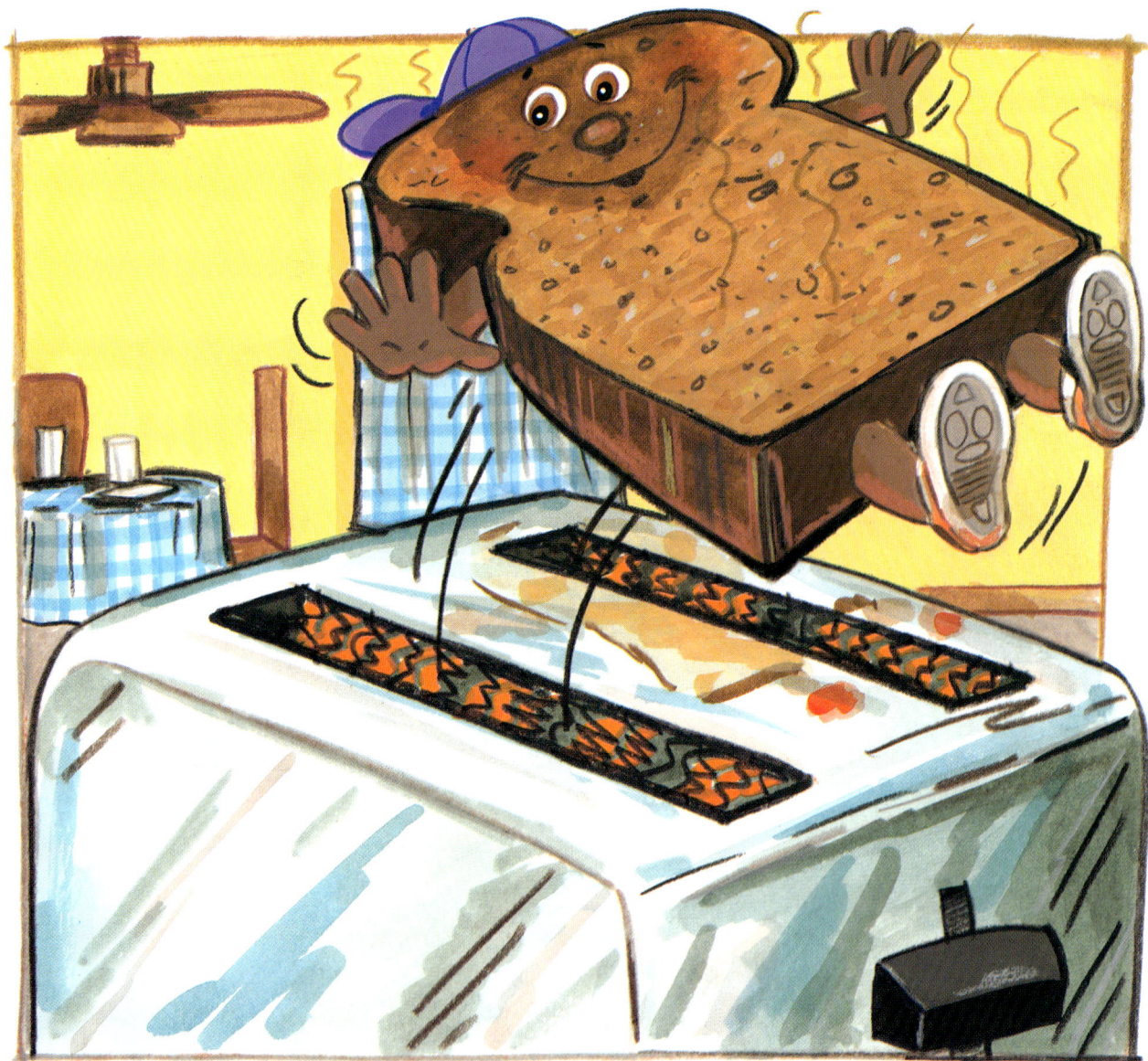

as warm as toast,

as flat as a pancake,

as sour as a lemon,

as hard as a rock,

as cold as ice,

as strong as an ox,

as quiet as a mouse,

as smart as a whip,

as deep as the ocean?

About the Author

Toni M. Egan earned her B.A. in English from CSU, Chico and her M.A. in Education from UC, Davis. She has taught in a classroom for 25 years and now teaches Reading Recovery™ at Bransford Elementary School in Fairfield, California. Toni lives in Davis, California with her husband and three children. She enjoys traveling and running.